friend indeed to us when we
were in deep need – Martin.

God Questions

...and some answers

Mike Hensman

Onwards and Upwards Publishers

Berkeley House,
11 Nightingale Crescent,
Leatherhead,
Surrey,
KT24 6PD,
United Kingdom.
www.onwardsandupwards.org

Printed in the UK by 4edge Limited.

ISBN: 978-1-910197-51-6
Typeface: Sabon LT
Graphic design: LM Graphic Design

Endorsements

"Mike Hensman has been a powerful witness for Jesus Christ for many years. It is typical of him that even now, when facing serious illness, he is still passionate about communicating God's love and grace far and wide."

Nicky Gumble
Creator of the Alpha Course
Vicar, Holy Trinity Brompton

"This book invites you to join a conversation with Mike Hensman, a minister of the United Reformed Church who has always been more interested in people outside the Church than in maintaining religious structures. If his questions are ones you ask, this book will give you straight, accessible answers about the Christian faith. Mike plunges fearlessly into longstanding theological debates and comes out with a clear steer. Nothing is off limits. Like his description of Mark's Gospel, he is 'short and punchy'. If sometimes his answers beg more questions, nobody would be more pleased than Mike if you were prompted to explore further."

John G. Ellis
Moderator of the General Assembly 2013-16
The United Reformed Church

God Questions

To all who wish to know more
about God,

especially those who do not want to
get caught up into "religion".

Contents

Foreword by Bishop Christopher Herbert...8

Introduction 9

1. What is It All about?...11

2. Is There a Spirit World?..12

3. What are Angels? 14

4. How Did Everything Begin? 16

5. How Did Life Come To Exist?...17

6. What is the Trinity? 18

7. What are Souls and Spirits?..20

8. The Fall: What Went Wrong? 22

9. What is Sin? 24

10. What is in the Bible? 26

11. What is The Jewish Law? 27

12. What about the Rest of the Old Testament? 29

13. What is in the New Testament? 31

14. Where is It All Leading? 33

15. What is God's Judgement Seat? 35

16. Does God Have a Rescue Plan? 37

17. Who was Jesus?..39

18. What Did Jesus Do? 41

19. What is Holy Week? 43

20. What Happened at the Crucifixion? 45

21. Was Jesus Really Resurrected?...47

22. What is the Good News? 49

23. How Can We Be Forgiven? 51

24. How Do We Deal With Guilt? 53

25. Can a Christian Be Demon-possessed? 55

26. Do Evil Spirits Exist? 57

27. Is there a Hell? 59

28. Is Heaven a Celestial Golf Course? 61

29. What is the Second Coming? 63

30. What is Meant By 'a New Heaven and a New Earth'? 64

31. Who is the Holy Spirit? 65

32. What Does the Holy Spirit Do? 67

33. What is Baptism in the Holy Spirit? 69

34. What is 'Walking in the Spirit'? 72

35. What is 'Fellowship in the Holy Spirit'? 74

36. What is the Church? 76

37. What is Water Baptism? 79

38. What is Holy Communion? 81

39. How Should I Pray? 83

40. Why is there Suffering in the World? 86

41. Does God Heal Today? 88

42. What is God's View of Sex? 90

43. So What Happens When You Believe? 91

44. What Does 'Grace' Mean? 93

45. What Does It Mean to Be 'In Christ'? 94

46. What is Witnessing? 96

Appendix One. Life to Share – Life in the Spirit 97

Appendix Two. 33 Bible Quotes that Apply to All Christians 99

Foreword

by Bishop Christopher Herbert

Some books are written from the outside, others are written from the inside. This is an *inside book.*

What do I mean by that? Well… this book has been written by author Mike Hensman in the knowledge that, because he has a serious illness, he probably does not have much longer to live. This has caused him to explore a number of Christian themes, not by *providing answers,* which is what a Christian minister might be expected to do, but by *asking questions.*

If you too are a questioner – and how can anyone claim to have faith if they have not questioned things seriously? – this book might well be one which will help you. It is designed to provoke conversations, to stimulate thinking, and ultimately to lead us to the greatest question of all, which is about the nature of God. It is only by exploring questions with diligence and simplicity of heart that any of us can hope to make progress.

Rt Revd Doctor Christopher Herbert, BA, MPhil, PhD
Retired Bishop of St Albans

Introduction

Hallo! My name is Mike. I am a Christian minister – I sometimes also get called a vicar or a priest – and I have a rare and incurable cancer which has been spreading through my body for nearly three years.

I have had a wonderful life, poor and rich, success and failure, quite well known locally, and often invited to preach and to lead courses on all manner of Christian subjects. I have enjoyed it and been good at it.

Much of my time has been with people outside the normal structures of the church. I work with a lot of people who feel they don't fit in and, in our culture, may not. I suppose I am a bit of a rebel.

My life has been very active and God has used it.

Then they discovered I have a large, inoperable brain tumour. I had to give up driving.

I was lying in an MRI scanner at the Royal Marsden Hospital, relaxed, in complete silence, not thinking of anything, just 'being', when God spoke to me.

"I want you to change the location of the ministry I have given you. I want you to minister, not out of strength but out of weakness and out of dependency on God and on other people."

This book is part of that. It is written for people who have questions. Who may not know anything about 'religion' – I hate that word – but who might want to know something about God.

It is also written for Christians wanting to help them with the answers. It does not claim to give all the answers in detail, but to invite further questions and discussion. It doesn't even try to be strictly grammatical. It does seek, as a first step, to reflect the answers that turn up in everyday conversations, in the hope that readers may wish to explore further.

God Questions

You will find quite a lot of overlap and repetition in the answers, simply because the same principles and ideas cover a multitude of subjects.

So, ask away.

QUESTION 1

What is It All About?

All of us, at some stage, will have had times of wondering what life is all about. There must be more than we can see.

It's about Jesus – God came to earth two thousand years ago – teaching, healing, and loving. Born as one of us, he grew and worked among people for three years and had more impact than any other human being in all time. A man of love, of truth, of wisdom.

A man on your side, who loved the lonely and the outcast. Who was angry only with those who oppressed the poor and acted all high and mighty.

A man who was rejected by the authorities of his time and tortured to the most terrible death of crucifixion. He was certified dead. And buried.

And three days later, he rose from the dead.

This is a fact of history, impossible but undeniable to anyone who approaches the evidence honestly.

A man who changed the world and everything in it. A man who loves you and wants to be your friend.

More anon, but we must start at the beginning.

QUESTION 2

Is There a Spirit World?

Throughout history, and worldwide in every civilisation, mankind has known there is 'something better' – something else – a spiritual dimension to life. It seems that this idea is a universal one built into the human psyche.

There are two worlds. There is the natural world that we experience and in which we live out our natural life span. The world we see.

And there is a spiritual world, supernatural, unseen, the dwelling place of God.

It is a world outside the confines of time and space. Everlasting – eternal.

In it live the spirits of all who have died and, in human terms, have 'gone to heaven'. A spirit can be defined as a person or being without a body. Also there are the angels – God's servants and messengers.

There is often an idea about a door in between the two worlds – a thin place where the spirit and natural worlds meet.

We sometimes may get glimpses of the unseen, such as when we look up at the enormity of a starlit sky and wonder at the glory of creation, or when we are captured by an experience of beautiful music. Flashes of joy and awesome wonder.

Jesus came through that door two thousand years ago to bring us back to God when we had got it all wrong.

Inevitably, we see *our* experience as the real one. We are trapped in it, and our 'afterlife' is seen as shadowy and rather scary. It may be that it would be better to think the other way round.

We were created to share with God his life in the unseen.

That is the real life. What we experience in this life, for all its beauty and wonders is only a 'before life' – a preparation for something infinitely more wonderful.

QUESTION 3

What are Angels?

Angels are spiritual beings, created by God, who dwell largely in the unseen world, although they can slip across the boundary into our world and back again, when they are going about their work as God's special servants. The word 'angel' means 'messenger'.

They are depicted as having some sort of ranking hierarchy and as having special roles; for example, the archangels – the best known being Gabriel, who announced the coming of Jesus into the world, and Michael, who is described as the commander of God's armies.

The Hebrew 'cherub' (plural 'cherubim') is a powerful creature with a flaming sword, set by God to guard the entrance to the Garden of Eden, to prevent man's re-entry after his disobedience right at the beginning of the Bible.

And there are 'seraphim', majestic creatures, praising God and before whose voices the whole earth shook.

They are very different from the rather soppy looking figures with wings and haloes depicted by medieval artists.

Angels are described as 'ministering spirits', appearing in all sorts of situations and in different disguises, not always recognised by the people they are sent to.

There is also a special title 'The Angel of the Lord', which seems to refer to a manifestation of God himself into our world.

When Jesus was born, the whole sky was filled with angels, praising God in a display that must have made the aurora borealis look like a flickering candle by comparison.

Angels fed Elijah in the Old Testament, when he was depressed and on the verge of giving up. Angels looked after Jesus, when he had been exhausted, after his forty day fast at the beginning of his ministry on earth.

There is a somewhat mysterious bit in the New Testament about the 'angels' of children always being before the Lord, which has led to the suggestion that every child has a 'guardian angel' – but that is not very clear.

It is also written that God will give his angels charge over us, to protect us and 'bear us up' if we fall, which may suggest guardian angels for us as well. (I, personally, have had a quite literal experience of this.)

There are also references to rebellious angels – evil characters resisting and fighting against God; but more of them elsewhere.

And, right at the end of the Bible, when God is putting everything to rights – a new heaven and a new earth – we have, around the throne of God, a vision of many angels, thousands of thousands, praising Jesus as worthy to receive power and wealth and wisdom and might and honour and glory and blessing for ever and ever. Wow! Amen!

QUESTION 4

How Did Everything Begin?

God is spirit. The source of all that is wonderful. God *is* love, all power, all peace, all life, all that is beautiful.

God is not bounded by time. He is eternal. God is not bounded by space or distance.

His power is infinite. His knowledge is infinite. God's dwelling is the unseen, uncreated world. The world of the Spirit.

And this amazing God created another world. Our world, the material world of space, of galaxies, and of Earth – the world that we live in.

QUESTION 5

How Did Life Come To Exist?

We don't know how God created the world – no one was there to see so there is no point in arguing about it.

God very rarely explains the *how* of his activity – we could not get our minds round it if he did. He does explain a lot about *why.*

He created a perfect world of beauty.

He loves us, he is excited by his creation, and he wants to share all that is wonderful – love, joy, peace – with us. He longs for our company and delights in our response. He is in love with us.

He has made us 'in his image' with his characteristics, including freewill. We have freedom to choose or reject the relationship he wants with us. A forced relationship is not love.

He has placed in us a longing for himself. The dweller in the Amazon rainforest, the desert Arab, and the most modern and science-led academic all share in knowing there is 'something more' – something outside – something to be reached for.

There are actually two stories at the beginning of the Bible, probably written with several hundred years between them and from slightly differing cultures, about the events of creation.

When this happens, it usually means that God wants the reader to pick up two different slants on what it he is getting at. They are put in very simple story form so all ages and civilisations can follow.

If you try to reconcile them into one story, it sometimes gets a bit fanciful. The trick is to ask what God wants you to learn out of each and both.

QUESTION 6

What is the Trinity?

You will have seen churches dedicated to the 'Holy Trinity'. Trinity means 'threesome'. You may have heard people talking about God as "one in three and three in one".

The word 'Trinity' does not appear in the Bible, but there is much evidence for its existence. All of which is very confusing, and some of the greatest minds in church history have tried to understand and explain it. Without success.

So we needn't worry too much if *we* can't.

God reveals to us only what we need to know. There is always an element of mystery. And we have to learn to trust.

There is only one God, and he has always existed. God created and sustains everything. The Bible opens with the words, "In the beginning, God..."

And yet we experience him as three 'persons' – God the Father, God the Son (Jesus) and God the Holy Spirit – each with his own separate role within the Godhead. All three were involved in creation.

God *is* love. All three are in such close intimacy and loving relationship with each other that they effectively operate as one – one in mind, one in power, one in purpose, one in wisdom, and one in everything.

The Father is constantly active, and Jesus, when he was on earth, never did anything unless he saw the Father doing it.

Jesus laid aside his 'godishness' to come to earth, as a man. He came to deal with all that separates us from God; to take away our sin; to restore our broken relationship with God; and to overcome death when he was raised from the dead.

He came to give us eternal life, sharing in the very love and life of the Godhead. He changed everything in mankind's relationship with God in preparation for the amazing 'new heaven and new earth', which is God's plan for the very end of time.

The Holy Spirit has been called the 'go-between God'. He is living constantly among us, and within all who believe. He is living constantly within the Godhead and working out God's purposes for us and all creation.

Still mystery? Things will get a bit clearer as we continue our exploration of what God has revealed.

QUESTION 7

What are Souls and Spirits?

Created in the image of God, we also are three in one. We have bodies, we have souls (the Greek root is the word 'psyche' – and its study 'psychology') and we have spirits.

Our spirit is our very core – the life that is in us – the life that relates to God. When the human race decided to go its own way, and ignore or disobey God, our spirits became effectively dead and sin entered in; we were cut off from God.

When we respond to God's invitation to receive his forgiveness and to accept Jesus as our Saviour, Master and Friend, our spirits come alive in a renewed relationship with Christ, which will end up in heaven.

Our body is more obvious. We all have them. We will look after them properly, or not. They will get sick and get better. They will respond to the ravages of time. And they will die.

But this is not the end for the Christian. We shall receive new bodies, spiritual bodies – like Jesus had after he rose from the dead. We don't know much about them and we don't need to. People in Jesus's time who wanted to know more were told in the Bible not to be so stupid. God knows – trust him.

Our soul is more complicated. Your soul is YOU – your intellect, your memories, your personality, your emotions, your will. Each of these elements has been affected by all sorts of influences, good and bad.

Our heredity, our early formative experiences from birth onwards, our education, our teenage development, our relationships, the choices we have made and things that have been done to us. The range is enormous. You are unique. And probably not a little messed up.

God has a remedy. One of the many wonderful things that happens to a new Christian is that the Holy Spirit – the Spirit of God – enters into them and begins a healing and clear-up programme, designed specifically for them. We may or may not recognise it. We may or may not be very cooperative. Different bits will take longer or shorter times. The process will take a lifetime.

But the end is that we shall arrive healed and transformed – ready and fit for our eternal life in and with Jesus.

QUESTION 8

The Fall: What Went Wrong?

God had created a perfect world – the Garden of Eden is another symbol.

Everything in perfect harmony. Mankind totally free, perfect relationships with all nature, especially between the sexes and between God and humankind. We were created to walk and talk, naked and unashamed, with God – perfect love, perfect sex (this, to some people's surprise, was God's first commandment!)

What of Adam and Eve, snakes and eating apples? No one was there to see but they are almost certainly symbolic pictures. They carry truth in them but you have to work it out.

They were designed to speak to all generations, all cultures, and all people throughout all time. Not just to our sophisticated lot.

We are talking about rebellion against God. People want to be like God – remember, we have his nature somehow wired into us. The problems were that people...

- ...were adding to God's word and putting in commands that didn't come from God;
- ...were disobeying God;
- ...thought they knew better than God;
- ...used the free choices given them by God to follow exciting temptations – not what God wanted for their own good.

God, actually, does know best.

And the results of these choices? Separation from God and the mess the world is now in.

This thing called *sin* takes over.

- We want our own way.
- We know best.
- *Me* first. *Me* (not God) at the centre.
- Sexuality is debased.
- Love becomes lust.
- The perfect relationship between man and nature is destroyed.

Pain, sickness and ultimately death are introduced into the world. From the account of early human history we get a picture of what the world was like.

Murder, getting worship wrong, violence, strange giant-like characters. People made discoveries and took up various new activities – hunter-gatherers emerged, farming started. People argued. People had to learn what worship pleased God.

And God knows. He loves his beautiful creation – and already has a rescue package in his mind to prevent us from getting into an even worse mess.

But we have to wait for his perfect timing before it all works out. We, the human race, have a lot to learn.

QUESTION 9

What is Sin?

SIN is a very terrible thing. We have trivialised it, as we usually do to things that we don't understand and that scare us.

We send defaulting rugby players to the 'sin bin'; we talk of the 'sinful' delights of that extra cream cake; we talk of 'little white lies'. Some people feel it necessary to try to recall and list every little 'sin' they can remember, so they can confess it and escape God's wrath. These 'sins' – notice the final 's' – may, or may not, trouble God very much.

But SIN is a very terrible thing.

It entered the world when mankind decided it knew better than God; we chose to ignore him, and got on with doing things our own way. It is rebellion against God. It is the natural state humanity chose when God gave us freewill. And it cuts us off from all that is good and beautiful, and from the relationship God longs to enjoy with us.

There was once a story about a man who had a little dog. He was a wicked little dog, who embodied everything that could be bad. His master called him 'Pagleas'.

- **P** for pride
- **A** for anger
- **G** for gluttony
- **L** for lust
- **E** for envy
- **A** for avarice
- **S** for sloth

We have all got bits of most of these, if not all, lurking within us somewhere. They are, in different combinations, the root of all wars, cruelty, oppression, torture, bullying and destruction of the planet.

There are seven terms in our Bible translations describing sin: unbelief, missing the mark, iniquity, transgression, trespass, error and lawlessness.

That is SIN and it leads to death. But God who loves us has provided a remedy.

QUESTION 10

What is in the Bible?

God gave us the Bible. Not a book, but a library of sixty-six books. All different. Written by people at God's prompting over a period of hundreds of years and containing all that God wants us to know about himself and his relationship with us.

It is an amazing library. Often in story form but all of it with deep meaning that can be understood in all cultures and all ages. It does not set out to be a scientific textbook but a way that God communicates with us. Is it a story or did it really happen like that? It often doesn't matter. God wants to speak to you through it.

It was originally written in mainly Hebrew and Greek.

There are many translations with slight differences, and we do not have any originals. It is God who does the interpreting, bringing his messages through it into our hearts and minds. Sometimes the same event or subject is approached in several different ways to help us hear what God is saying. But in every story, God is active.

This library has two shelves.

- The 'New Testament', starting perhaps in AD 45, by people who had known Jesus or been close to events.
- The other shelf, the Hebrew Scriptures – our 'Old Testament' – is the one Jesus was brought up on. It was written anything up to three thousand years ago, although some of the stories are even older.

QUESTION 11

What is The Jewish Law?

The first five books of the Bible, known to Judaism as 'The Law', form the basis of the Jewish faith, setting out stories and information from ancient times. After the creation stories, there are things like Noah's Ark and loads of family histories.

The five books record religious experiences and practices in the history of Israel and set out rules for living. Many of these rules seem to have sprung from current local issues but all are taken as directly from God – and they are a very mixed bag.

There are hundreds of them, ranging from the Ten Commandments to a prohibition on eating prawns (they can give you food poisoning, if you are wandering in a desert without a fridge).

They required absolute obedience, and a terrible curse was laid on anyone who did not obey the lot.

If your son is rebellious, you have to make an application to the local authority and say, "My son is rebellious," and they will arrange for him to be stoned to death. If you want to sell your daughter into slavery, it tells you how to do it. And you must not move your neighbour's boundary fence.

They are often quoted nowadays completely out of context. "An eye for an eye and a tooth for a tooth" is not an invitation to revenge but is a limitation of punishment in a primitive society, where any wrongdoing was likely to be avenged by killing.

You will still hear people saying, "The Bible says…" to justify almost anything but you do have to understand the context.

God Questions

There are also some beautiful and exciting passages talking about how God loves and provides for his people.

There are ceremonials, holidays and festivals that cement and give structure to society, a bit like Christmas, Easter and school holidays do for us.

You probably don't need to know all this if you are new to faith – it's probably not the best place to start your reading, but it can be interesting.

QUESTION 12

What about the Rest of the Old Testament?

After the first five books of the Law, there follow twelve books of the history of the Israelite nation in their journey with God. Good kings, bad kings, battles won, battles lost; obedience to God and ignoring him and the consequences for the nation.

And then four called the Wisdom Literature – ideas assembled from a variety of sources from some of the greatest philosophers of the time, including a very beautiful, erotic poem about the courtship of the lover and the beloved – a picture of the courtship of God and his people.

After the first of these is inserted the book of Psalms – the hymn book of the ancient temple in Jerusalem. There are a hundred and fifty songs, which cover every possible human response to God. You can always find one which puts into words how you are feeling towards God. You will find every aspect of human life there – joy, comfort, misery, guilt, longing, worship, anger with God, the lot – and they will bring you nearer to him.

Perhaps the best known is the 23rd Psalm – 'The Lord's my Shepherd'.

As a teenager once put it, adapting the Mars Bar advert, "A psalm a day helps you work, rest and pray."

Then come the prophets, who, with the Law, form the two pillars of Old Testament faith.

A prophet is not some sort of sacred fortune teller, but a person inspired by God to bring his message to his people. Forth-telling, not primarily foretelling, although some of them do describe things that are to come.

There are three 'major prophets', magnificent writers – Isaiah, Jeremiah and Ezekiel – whose work continues to be totally relevant to us today. In talking about God as they knew him, they were often talking about Jesus who was to come.

And finally there are thirteen 'minor prophets' – shorter books, most of them addressing problems of their own time and giving God's reactions, encouragements and warnings.

That's the Old Testament, completed some 2,500 years ago. It is a fascinating study of ancient sociology, psychology and a primitive society emerging into a civilisation; with God steering through thick and thin to provide exactly the right setting to come into for the rescue of humanity – coming to us in Jesus.

And he loves you.

QUESTION 13

What is in the New Testament?

In these twenty-seven books we find most of what we know about Jesus and all we need to know about living as Christians in the new life Jesus won for us on the cross.

It starts with the four books called 'gospels' – the old English word for 'good news'. They were written by different people, each from a slightly different point of view.

Matthew comes from a Jewish background; Mark, short and punchy, seems to be almost out of breath while trying to capture the major events they had lived through. Luke was sent, a bit like a modern investigative journalist, to report back to his sponsor in Greece.

There is evidence that these three had seen each other's work, as there is some overlap. John's gospel, written maybe fifty years later, contains much of the early churches' experience of living in the new life in the power of the Holy Spirit.

It is from the four gospels that we know all that God wants us to know about Jesus's life and ministry on earth.

There is then another book, also by Luke about the Holy Spirit moving in the early church with miracles and great power. It is called Acts, or Acts of the Apostles.

Enter a man called Paul. A brilliant man, steeped in Judaism, full of hatred for Christians and wanting nothing more than to persecute and kill any he could find.

He had been given a warrant by the Jewish authorities and was on his way, with a group of followers, from Jerusalem to Damascus to do just that. And on the way he had an amazing meeting with the risen Jesus, who asked him why he was persecuting him. Paul was so blinded by the glory of Jesus that he had to be led into the city where he, the arch-enemy of the church, received healing in the church.

We then lose sight of him for three years, during which he undergoes a total change of heart and mind and becomes the greatest Christian writer of the age.

In the early days of their new faith, Christians gathered in small groups of people dispersed around the Roman Empire. They did not have the written gospels or any trained leadership. They faced a mass of different issues about their new life, forgiveness, whether you had to obey the Jewish Law and, if so, which bits? And so on. News would come back to Paul and he would write back giving them answers. We don't always know the questions.

We have nine of his replies to these new churches and four to individuals, making up much of the New Testament. The books are named by their destinations, e.g. Romans to the church in Rome, Corinthians to Corinth, Galatians to the region of Galatia. We also have four personal letters giving advice to local church leaders, and seven letters written by other people to different destinations, usually named in the first few verses.

Nobody knows who wrote the letter to the Hebrews.

There are people who say they will believe what Jesus says but not the things written by 'only Paul'. A great mistake. Paul's letters do need to be understood in their context. But they share with us his unique experience of the Holy Spirit working in his life, as the Holy Spirit longs to work in ours.

And finally there is the book entitled Revelation – quite different from anything else in the Bible. That, we will look at next.

QUESTION 14

Where is It All Leading?

The last book of the Bible is Revelation. Also known as the Apocalypse, meaning 'unveiling'. A vision, a God-given fantasia, some of it in weird symbolism, written by a disciple named John in exile for his faith on the Aegean island of Patmos. It looks forward to the end of creation as we know it. It is a revelation from God about the new heaven and new earth that he will create after Jesus has returned to earth in all his glory. John is told to write it and send it to the churches.

Almost inevitably, it has been much argued over. Some say the events have already happened – they quite obviously haven't – and try to match it with known history. Some can't handle the symbolism.

Like much prophecy, it is probably best seen as applying to the time when it was given, to the near future and to the long term future – us.

Chapters 2 and 3 are reasonably straightforward – praise and criticism to seven churches in Asia, which also apply to many churches, even today.

The next 15 chapters become more difficult. The story alternates between what is happening in the heavens – the unseen – and on the earth – the seen. And the symbolism becomes more controversial.

There are dragons and weird multi-headed monsters. Are these to be taken literally? Do they represent enemy countries? Is 'Babylon' a code word for 'Rome'? What is the sinister sign '666'? You can see why theologians argue.

You will hear some Christians saying the world is going to get better and better as we try to build God's kingdom on earth. This is exactly the opposite of what these chapters say. They describe terrible situations on earth – famine, disease, war between nations and between Satan and God, earthquakes, persecution and the very stars falling from the heavens.

All this for a period of seven years called the Great Tribulation, as the fallout of a monumental battle, which rages to and fro between the angelic army and Satan's spiritual forces in the unseen world. The earthly battle ends in Israel at the village called the Hill of Megiddo – Ha Megiddo in Hebrew – Armageddon.

We have been repeatedly told, including by Jesus, that no one except God the Father knows when this is all going to happen. But look at your TV news and you might see some similarities.

So read it, a bit at a time. Use your imagination about the situations described, and ask God to show you what he is saying to you through it.

Move on to chapter 19 – a mixture of hope, promise and judgement. The war is ended, the Lord our God Almighty reigns. And there is the great marriage feast, with the church as the bride and Jesus as the groom.

QUESTION 15

What is God's Judgement Seat?

There is a theme of God's judgement running through the whole Bible. God is a God of love, his mercy triumphs over his wrath, but he is also a God of justice.

In the Old Testament, we have a picture where every misfortune of his people was interpreted as God's punishment for disobedience and lack of faith. The idea of a punishing God to be feared has somehow stuck.

In the New Testament, there is a much more balanced teaching. People who know God's laws but soak themselves in all manner of evil deserve to die.

God's kindness is meant to lead to repentance.

At the end of time, when earth and sky are no more, we have a picture of a great white throne.

Every one, in the last days, shall appear before this judgement throne of God to receive according to his works, to receive eternal life or wrath and fury.

In passing, you may hear some false teaching that only 144,000 people will be saved. This figure in the book of Revelation is a symbolic one, referring to the twelve tribes of Israel. This teaching completely ignores the bit that follows: "...and a great multitude that no man could number from every nation..."

All who have received the Jewish Law will be judged by standards of the Law.

So what about people who have never heard of the Law or of Jesus? When they do good, they will be in a special category. They will show that what the Law requires is written on their hearts. God judges the deepest secrets of our hearts.

And God always gets it right.

We are told not to judge other people because (a) we don't know all the facts and (b) we would, ourselves, deserve the same condemnation if Jesus had not rescued us.

God always gets it right.

In one place, Jesus gives a slightly ambiguous teaching – it is not clear whether it applies to individuals, nations or both. In the final judgement, Jesus says, it will be like a shepherd separating the sheep from the goats on a basis of how they treated the hungry, the poor, the stranger. Jesus commends the sheep saying that, wittingly or without knowing it, their compassion was directed to him. The goats, who did not do likewise, would go to eternal punishment.

There are also special rewards (the Bible talks of 'crowns') for steadfastness, perseverance, devotion to Christ, soul winners, feeders of God's sheep, and suffering.

At the throne, the account books will be opened and the dead judged by what they have done.

But... there is another book which often slips attention – THE LAMB'S BOOK OF LIFE – in which are written the names of all who have believed in Jesus; they already have eternal life and all the blessings of heaven.

Question 16

Does God Have a Rescue Plan?

God has a plan, to restore the whole of creation into a new heaven and a new earth at the end of time. A new and perfect creation, and a new and perfect relationship with him.

He has been intervening and steering in human history like a wise parent with a wayward teenager. There is a hymn: "God is working his purpose out as year succeeds to year."

He chose a people – a nation – especially for this purpose. He chose a godly man, Abraham, as the father of the nation, the Hebrew people – the Jewish race.

He taught them and trained them in his ways over the centuries and eventually gave them a vision of a great 'leader' – the Jewish term 'messiah' meaning 'chosen and anointed' – empowered by God. The Greek word for 'messiah' is Christos – Christ.

Messiah would come at exactly the right moment into exactly the right setting. And so it happened two thousand years ago.

The Jewish people were able to contribute their understanding of God. The Greek civilisation had developed many great philosophers and a thirst for wisdom and meaning. The Roman civilisation had produced (albeit briefly) a time of peace and the rule of law. Equally important were the Roman postal service and safe travel, enabling God's message to spread throughout the known world.

The conditions were exactly right.

God Questions

And God himself came from the unseen world into our world, into our time and space, to change everything and inaugurate a new relationship between mankind and God.

He came as a man, a man called *Jesus*.

QUESTION 17

Who was Jesus?

Jesus, Son of God in heavenly places – the unseen world – was instrumental in the very beginning in creation.

Looking back at the Jewish writings you can see dozens – if not hundreds – of references, sometimes hidden, to Jesus coming into our world and what would happen.

The four main references in the ancient Christian writing about why he came are:

- to take away the sin of the world;
- to destroy the works of the evil one (the devil);
- to set us free from the curse of the Law (having to earn God's favour);
- to establish a new basis for our relationship with God (a new Covenant of Love between God and humankind); in effect, to reverse the Fall.

The story begins with a strange tale of an angel visiting a young girl in Nazareth and telling her she has been chosen to have a baby by the Holy Spirit, a baby who will therefore have two natures: human and God's. And he will be the saviour of the world. The girl, Mary, agrees. People have been arguing about this bit ever since, trying to understand. Don't get caught up in the arguments.

Jesus was born in a stable in Bethlehem, the family's ancestral home, where they had gone to register at a census.

The king had tried to murder Jesus out of jealousy, and so the family became refugees in Egypt until the king died, when they returned to Nazareth where he was brought up.

We hear of two incidents in his childhood. The first being a visit to the temple in Jerusalem, where two godly people attested to who the baby was. The second is when he was around twelve and was clearly beginning to understand something about his relationship with the Father.

He remained in Nazareth, working as a carpenter.

Fast-forward to the age of about thirty when Jesus goes for baptism, is baptised and the Holy Spirit comes upon him – releasing God's power into him for the tasks that lie before him. He retreats into the desert for forty days to fast, pray and work it all out.

We shall be looking in detail later on at what followed.

QUESTION 18

What Did Jesus Do?

We can't be certain how long Jesus's earthly ministry lasted – probably about three years, which he spent walking the country towns and villages, particularly in Galilee, with visits to Jerusalem for the festivals. He had with him twelve chosen friends – his disciples (apprentices).

He was there to show people what God – whom no one has ever seen – was like.

He came especially to bring God's love to the poor, the down-trodden, the sick, the prostitutes and sinners, who were despised by the 'good' people. People flocked to him in their thousands.

In the power of the Holy Spirit, he fed people who were hungry. He healed the sick – over forty occasions are recorded, some of individuals, some of massive crowds, where he healed all who needed it. He raised three people from the dead.

He taught people about how God wanted them to live their lives. He did this largely by parables – made-up stories challenging people to think about, and remember, the sometimes hidden meaning.

You have probably heard of the parable of the Good Samaritan, for one.

He performed miracles, turning water into wine, calming a storm, walking on water, enabling his disciples to catch an enormous lot of fish after an exhausting night catching nothing.

All the time he was showing people the Kingdom of God.

And he said some amazing things about himself, which got him accused of blasphemy.

- He said he never did anything unless he saw his Father God doing it.
- He made seven statements starting "I am", indicating his Godhead, and a claim that he and the Father were one.
- He also said, "I and the Father are one," and, "Before Abraham was, I am."

He broke the religious rules and the authorities didn't like it. It was a unique ministry, unlike anything before or since. All of it demonstrating God's love and care for his people.

He was arrested as a troublemaker, tortured, put to death by crucifixion, rose again from the dead, and returned to his Father in the unseen world, where he now reigns over all creation as King of Kings and Lord of Lords.

A well-known Christian writer in the twentieth century, commenting on all the evidence, wrote about Jesus that he could only be one of three things. Either Jesus was mad, or he was bad, or he was actually and really, who he said he was: the Son of God. What do *you* think?

QUESTION 19

What is Holy Week?

And now the scene is set for the greatest battle ever fought in the two worlds – the seen and the unseen.

Jesus has raised from the dead a friend called Lazarus, in a little village just over the brow of the Mount of Olives from Jerusalem.

Tens of thousands of Jews, from throughout the known world, have come to Jerusalem for the Passover festival and are camped on the slopes of the Mount of Olives, facing the city. The Lazarus story would have been well known among them.

Thousands of people in the land believe in Jesus as the long-awaited Messiah – their deliverer.

The corrupt religious authorities fear and hate Jesus and want to be rid of him but are too afraid of the people.

The Roman governor, a weak man, is afraid of violent demonstrations and possible insurrection. He and the Jewish authorities are, unwillingly, in league with each other.

And on what we celebrate as Palm Sunday, Jesus comes into Jerusalem, riding on a donkey (a lowly animal) accompanied by vast crowds from the Mount of Olives hailing him as the Messiah.

The authorities plot to kill Jesus and Lazarus.

Jesus goes into the temple and finds it bustling with corrupt money changers and sellers of animals for sacrifice. We see his anger at their desecration of God's house. Making a whip, he drives them out. And still the authorities are too afraid of the people to take any action.

In the days that follow, he teaches openly in the temple. The authorities make a deal with Judas – one of the disciples – that he will show them where they can arrest Jesus without stirring the crowd.

On a day we celebrate as Maundy Thursday, Jesus has his Passover meal with the disciples and returns late at night to the garden at the foot of the Mount of Olives. Jesus, knowing what is going to happen, goes through a long period of agonising prayer. The disciples sleep. Jesus submits to his Father's will.

Judas arrives with soldiers, kisses Jesus. Jesus is arrested and taken to three tribunals – the last of which is Roman – the only one able to sentence to death. There are false witnesses; the chief priests inflame the crowd. They threaten Pilate the governor, who finds Jesus 'not guilty'. Nonetheless, in response to the baying crowd, he sentences Jesus to be flogged and crucified.

QUESTION 20

What Happened at the Crucifixion?

The authorities took Jesus out of the city to a place of execution and there crucified him, stripped naked, nailed through hands and feet to a wooden cross and left to die – a most barbaric form of execution. People had been known to take two or three days to die despite the heat, the flies and the vultures. Two criminals were crucified with him, one on each side. The execution squad and the public looked on.

And Jesus prayed for their forgiveness. The crowd and one of the thieves taunted him. The other thief recognised who he was and asked to be remembered when Jesus came into his kingdom. Jesus replied that he would remember and had a place waiting for him in heaven.

On the cross, 'Jesus took my sins away', 'Jesus took the punishment for all my sins', 'Jesus paid my ransom price' – Christian truths. He came to fulfil the Old Covenant relationship between God and mankind and to establish the New Covenant – one of grace and love and forgiveness – by the shedding of his blood. He came to offer this for each one of us who would believe.

But it also goes deeper than that.

Behind the battle for each of us, there hides the monumental, galactic battle that was being fought out as the Son of God, the sinless one, was fighting with evil – one of the purposes for which he came to be one of us on earth.

He took our sin upon himself, and died – and our sin died with him.

He accepted the dreadful Old Testament curse on anyone who broke any of the Law, and died – and the curse died with him.

He overcame Satan and death to open the kingdom of heaven to all believers.

And all of this was being fought out on the cross, to the point where he knew he had been forsaken by his Father in his total identification with sinful humanity. Satan seemed to have won.

As Jesus died, he cried out in triumph that his task had been accomplished, and committed his spirit to the Father.

They certified his death and took his dead body to a nearby tomb, and the authorities placed a guard and a seal on a great stone blocking the entrance to the tomb, for fear Jesus's followers might interfere.

Then, two days later... Read on!

QUESTION 21

Was Jesus Really Resurrected?

Everyone knew Jesus was *dead* and buried. His friends were hiding away, afraid they would be next. Two or three women went, early in the morning, to the tomb to embalm his body – feeling rather stupid because of the sealed tomb and the guards.

When they get there... no guards; the stone door rolled away; the tomb empty, except for the grave clothes. An angel asks, "Why seek the living among the dead?" And there Jesus meets them and they have a conversation.

The women go to the disciples, who don't believe them. Two of them go to the tomb and return mystified.

Meanwhile, two other disciples are leaving the city for a nearby village, and Jesus meets them on the road and explains everything – but they don't recognise him until they are having supper together and he breaks the bread. Then Jesus vanishes. They return hurriedly to Jerusalem and the disciples' hideout.

There the risen Jesus comes in through the locked door, shows them his scars, and asks for some food. He has a new body – real, touchable, but not bounded by time or space. *A resurrection body.*

He breathes on the disciples, he gives and they receive the Holy Spirit, and he says he is sending them out as the Father has sent him, to continue his ministry – but only after they have received power, when the Holy Spirit has come upon them.

In the next forty days there are many meetings with Jesus including the disciples, and one meeting of five hundred people at once.

Back in Jerusalem, the disciples and Jesus return to the Mount of Olives where Jesus leaves them, and a cloud receives him out of their sight. This is celebrated in the church as Ascension Day. He has returned to the heavens, whence he came, having completed his task on earth.

A few days later, the Holy Spirit comes upon the disciples, as Jesus promised, and they are transformed with power to go and preach the good news of God to the whole known world.

Can we believe this? It's a truth that is as well attested as the existence of William the Conqueror. If it is all a lie, it is the biggest fraud of all time.

And the very idea doesn't even begin to meet any legal probability test, since...

- nothing is impossible for God;
- Jesus had said it would happen;
- the most powerful occupying army in the world and all the religious authorities in the land would have done anything to deny the resurrection and find that body;
- the disciples were demoralised and hiding for fear that they were themselves next on the list (in no position to organise a fraud);
- there were many surviving witnesses over the next few years;
- the disciples were transformed from an assorted group of frightened semi-believers into a force that changed the world civilisations;
- the story is too wild for anyone to make it up(!);
- and we, today, can and do still meet the risen Christ, through the Holy Spirit.

Christ is alive. The last enemy – death – has been defeated. Wow!

QUESTION 22

What is the Good News?

The first written reference to the good news in the New Testament is when Jesus says, "The time you have all been waiting for has arrived; the Kingdom of God is at hand on earth." God the all wise, the all loving, the all powerful is in complete control of everything.

It doesn't always seem like it, but God's ways and thoughts in the unseen world are not the same as ours in the seen. His are better! We need new ways and new thinking to experience what he is doing in our messy and broken world.

God has opened the Kingdom of heaven to all believers.

If you believe in Jesus you have (immediately) everlasting life.

You are a child of God.

All your sin and guilt are taken away.

Satan and all the powers of evil and death have been defeated (although they are still fighting a rearguard action).

We are set free from trying to be good enough to 'go to heaven'. We never could be good enough to earn our place there, nor will we ever be too bad to get there – it is God's free gift, paid for by Jesus, to all who are willing to accept it and believe in him.

God is moving towards the end of the age when Jesus will return and everything will be made new – perfect.

Why? God loves all of his creation. Maybe he is so bursting with love that he had to share it. Maybe that is what creation was all about. That he wanted Jesus to fill heaven with the spirits of those who love him and belong to him. Perhaps he just wanted to bring glory to Jesus. We may never know until we meet him.

But we can choose to live our lives in amazed thankfulness – and rejoice.

God loves you.

QUESTION 23

How Can We Be Forgiven?

You will have heard the saying 'forgive and forget' and probably found this extremely difficult, if someone has really wronged you. In fact, it is not possible. We tend not to forget but to bury the hurt inside ourselves.

A Christian definition of forgiveness of someone who has hurt us is 'living with the memory but without holding it against them'. It is only God who has promised to forget.

All that we have ever done against God or other people – all our failures to do good – have *been* forgiven by God, when Jesus died on the cross and took away our sin.

Christians are forgiven people in God's eyes, and this is something we can rejoice in.

We need to know this for real, if we are to spread the good news of God's love and goodness to those around us. God does not condemn. We have no right to.

Knowing God's forgiveness for us is often linked with forgiveness in other ways.

If we have wronged anyone, we need to go and talk to them, asking their forgiveness, if this can be done without making things worse.

Incidentally, if the person you have harmed is dead, you can still ask their forgiveness – but *not* directly from them, because you should never try contact with the dead. Instead, you ask Jesus to handle it for you.

We may need to forgive anyone who has wronged us – whether or not we think they 'deserve it'. And they don't have to ask.

We don't deserve to be forgiven by God. We are forgiven only through his great love for us and because Jesus paid the price for our sin on the cross.

Failure to forgive builds up bitterness in us – a poison that gets in the way of our walk with God and our relationships with other people. We are called to love, even our enemies. Forgiving others releases them from whatever they have done to us.

Finally, and perhaps most hard, we have to forgive ourselves. Stop holding on to, "Aren't I awful?" or, "My sin is too bad." (Satan's lies)

Take hold of truth: *you are forgiven.*

There is some suggestion in the Bible that unless we forgive others, we cannot be forgiven by God, and the translations of the various fragments of early documents are of little help. But there is clearly a connection between forgiving and being forgiven.

This is probably best understood as meaning that if we are harbouring unforgiveness in our hearts, we shall not be able to receive and comprehend the forgiveness that we have received from God.

So, what can we do about it? We can openly accept the bitterness and grudges we continue to hold, instead of minimising them and saying, "Oh, it's OK, I've forgotten all about that." And ask God to deal with them.

If we don't recognise what is happening, we can ask the Holy Spirit to show us and to replace our bitterness with his love.

We can share with other Christians our problem and listen to what God may be saying through them to us. We can seek understanding of why the other person is like they are – and pray for their healing.

This may not be easy but nothing is impossible for God.

QUESTION 24

How Do We Deal With Guilt?

If you have become a Christian, God has forgiven all your sin. All, all, ALL!

Has forgiven. Jesus *has* set us free. So why do we so often feel guilty?

There are a number of reasons, and for each one there is a different way of dealing with it.

- There is the prompting of the Holy Spirit, when he is trying to show us something wrong in our lives, so we can get it right again. Any prompting from the Holy Spirit is gentle, and it can always be overlooked or shut out, if we are not open to him. It may be very persistent, however, because God never gives up on anyone. So listen to him, accept what he is saying, know God's forgiveness for it, and ask him to change you.
- The other spiritual source of guilt is the accusation of Satan. This is often harsh, sneering and damaging to your relationship with God. This has to be dealt with as the Bible teaches. Satan is an accuser and a liar. Rebuke and resist him, firm in the truth that you are a child of God, that your sin is taken away and that Satan is a defeated foe. And then stop looking at Satan, and move into praising Jesus for what he has done for you.

If the feelings persist you may need healing prayer or ministry from a trusted Christian counsellor or minister.

- A lot of guilt feelings come to us from our past experiences. We may have had very strict parents, who got at us and made us feel we were bad and unloved. It is almost as if the parent goes on living inside us, telling us off. This needs recognising and, probably, also needs prayer for healing.

- A variant of the parent is where we may have done some particular thing that we feel was very wicked when we were children. Perhaps we stole something or experienced some sexual act – either of our own doing or of something done to us. Again there is the need for healing prayer, often called 'healing of the memories', where the Holy Spirit is asked to come into the situation, as if it were still happening. He always will, and will 'make it better'.
- Then there is social guilt when other people push guilt into us – the pot calling the kettle black. Probably the best way of dealing with this is to make a special point of praying for them in their need.

When we feel guilty, we can make a conscious choice to rejoice in being children of God – forgiven, loved, and free, clothed in the righteousness of Christ. This is how God sees his sons and daughters for whom his Son died – so perhaps we should see things that way too.

Does God punish our sins by letting bad things happen? No. But he often does not let us get away without experiencing the natural and obvious consequences of what we have done. This is one of the ways he trains us and guides us for the future. He will discipline us, always in love.

The word 'confession' only means 'acknowledging' – not 'dodging' our faults. It has had a chequered history among Christians. At its worst, we have had priests denying people communion unless they come to the priest first with a long list of their sins, receive some sort of punishment, and then have their forgiveness pronounced in God's name.

We are told to confess our sins to one another, particularly if we are in need of healing, which need may result from the sin. In a loving, trusting fellowship this can be a real release.

Some people find it helpful, if troubled by guilt, to write why. The paper can then be given to God – perhaps by placing it on an altar, shredding it or burning it.

Once again, *you are forgiven*. Do you still want to feel guilty?

QUESTION 25

Can a Christian Be Demon-possessed?

There is a mysterious power of evil operating in the spirit world, seeking to disrupt God's work. This is scary. Some churches deny it. We shall see, later, God has already dealt with it.

Those with eyes to see know a power of evil is still rampant in our world. In the unseen world a cosmic battle rages. The result of the conflict is wars, pain, fear and all that is horrible and in opposition to a loving God.

People, particularly in earlier years, tried to make mock of this power to relieve their fear of it. Hence the pantomime idea of a devil with horns and a tail or other medieval pictures.

The Bible talks of rebel angels. Evil is personified in a spiritual being named Satan (literally the Accuser) or the devil, whose foot soldiers are demons or "unclean spirits".

They are a defeated foe but still don't lie down. And are very real. They are very subtle; liars, deceivers and murderers. Demons may attack people or churches. They may cause illness. They will do anything they can to frustrate God's plans.

Jesus had many encounters with demonic spirits in his time on earth. He gave power to his disciples to deal with them. People suffering under the power of unclean spirits were set free.

People who dabble in occult practices, even apparently innocent ones like ouija or magic charms, can still find themselves getting hooked. It is a dangerous business.

God Questions

And Jesus continues today his work of setting people free through the healing ministry of his church in the power of the Holy Spirit.

QUESTION 26

Do Evil Spirits Exist?

This is a strange subject. It is hard for the scientific western culture to comprehend – and perhaps the more dangerous for that.

All other cultures and all periods of history recognise evil forces, the weird, the unexplained, and the spiritual.

Jesus, the Bible, and the church throughout the ages have taught that we are in a state of spiritual warfare.

The Holy Spirit has been poured on to the church and many people are experiencing this.

Likewise Satan, the devil, the adversary of God – call him what you like – is alive and active. He will do everything he can to keep people from God – now and in all eternity.

Evil has been defeated by the shed blood of Jesus, but Satan is still fighting a rearguard action. Evil spirits – often called demons – are Satan's army.

No true Christian can be possessed by evil spirits; a Christian is possessed by the Holy Spirit. But he can have a demon lurking inside (sometimes called being 'demonised') or be harassed, influenced, attacked and, perhaps more often than many imagine, made ill by them. Irrational fears, emotional states or bizarre behaviour may have a psychiatric cause. They may also be demonic. Or both.

Discernment is essential.

No Christian need ever be afraid of evil spirits, and Jesus's victory on the cross over Satan is given to Christians also.

Setting people free (often called deliverance ministry) is part of the ministry of the church. Jesus's disciples were given authority to cast out demons – as Spirit-filled Christians have been today. But it is not a ministry to be trifled with, and not for the inexperienced.

Evil spirits are interlopers. They have no authority to come into a person, much less to stay, unless (sometimes unwittingly) they are given an opening – a 'landing pad' – or invited in. This may happen if a person wilfully opposes God's laws.

Another very common 'invitation' is where a person has had anything to do with the occult – mediums, witchcraft, fortune telling, ouija, astrology, divining, trying to contact the dead or other spiritual practices.

People often dabble, saying there is no harm in this, and lay themselves open to the most awful spiritual consequences. They are disobeying all God's teaching, which strictly forbids such practices.

Possession or attack may not always be the sufferer's fault, especially if their family have been involved in any form of Satan worship or witchcraft.

Every case is different, and the Holy Spirit gives understanding and discernment to deliverance ministers.

If you want to know more, ask a minister or pastor about all this. But not all have a calling in this area; if they feel they have not, ask God to show you someone who will be able to help. And he will.

QUESTION 27

Is there a Hell?

Most of the common ideas about hell come from folklore and not scripture.

In the Old Testament the beliefs about the afterlife were shadowy. Dead people went to 'Sheol' (the Greek 'Hades'), a place of the dead, not particularly a place of punishment.

The Bible also talks of 'Gehenna' as the part of Sheol reserved for the wicked. This was the valley of Hinnom outside Jerusalem, which was the rubbish dump, where there were always fires burning and where children had been sacrificed to false gods.

In medieval times there were all sorts of lurid images of hell – pitchforks for pushing the wicked into flames, dogs eating your feet if you had danced too much, and the like.

There was also the idea of purgatory – a waiting place where souls might be purged before final judgement. This is not a biblical idea and denies the complete cleansing and salvation through faith in Jesus.

So what happens to those who die not belonging to Jesus or who refuse his new life for whatever reason?

There are Christians who say that God is too kind and loving to reject anybody, and say that everyone will end up in heaven. *But* this is *not* what Jesus said.

Hell has been described as where God is not. Ultimately, God cannot stop you from refusing him if that is your set will.

We can't be too dogmatic, but the Bible gives some frightening clues.

God Questions

Jesus speaks a terrifying denunciation of the self-righteous, hypocritical 'good guys' of his time. Clean and respectable on the outside but rotten on the inside. Particularly those who oppress the poor and defenceless.

He says they will go away to eternal punishment; he uses words like 'just retribution' and 'place of torment'. It is a separation from God – a place where the wicked of this world and Satan and all his demons... meet.

He tells a story, teaching that once you are in, you can't get out.

God will *judge*. He is God of *Mercy*. Also of *Justice*.

Jesus offers *eternal life*.

You have the choice.

QUESTION 28

Is Heaven a Celestial Golf Course?

Most of the ideas people have about heaven are not from the Bible, but hangovers from pagan or pre-Christian belief.

The word 'paradise' originally referred to a beautiful garden – perhaps going back to the Garden of Eden.

The New Testament does not say much about where paradise is or what happens there. People throughout time have tried to fathom the mystery.

Folk culture, which is widely believed, is that 'heaven' is a place of resting in peace or standing round God's throne for all eternity singing praise (must be pretty boring).

Or, perhaps, even a permanent golf course for golf enthusiasts. Or meeting our old granny again. All these seem to reflect our earthly understanding – they are based on human desires. They may bring comfort but they trivialise the wonder of God's promises almost out of existence.

Jesus did say to his friends that in God's house there are many places – the old translations of the Bible say "many mansions" – and that he was going to prepare places for them.

He promised paradise to a criminal being executed beside him.

Christianity is not about where heaven is. It is about relationship with God through Jesus, in the unseen world.

It is about being in love and loved, about being forgiven and made perfect. It is about never fearing, about overcoming death and being healed.

God Questions

It is about being with Jesus for ever and experiencing a greater love, joy and peace than we can possibly imagine.

If you believe in Jesus, you will be sharing his life and his glory.

You will have a new celestial body – no more pain, sickness or aging.

Jesus is going to return to earth at the end of time. And you, Christian, will be there, with him for ever.

QUESTION 29

What is the Second Coming?

In the Old Testament, there are constant references to the 'great and terrible day of the Lord' who will come, with great might, as deliverer for his people.

Jesus did come – but as the suffering servant, in humility, lowliness and love to rescue and save humanity. This they did not expect.

The Christian church proclaims as the centre of its faith, "Christ has died, Christ is risen, Christ will come again."

When Jesus ascended to heaven after the resurrection, angels appeared to the mystified disciples and told them that he would come again in the same way they had seen him go.

The New Testament talks of Jesus coming again, with great power and all the glory of God, and with angels gathering all his 'elect' – people, dead and alive – to meet him in the air and be with him for ever.

The term 'elect' has caused all sorts of trouble. Are some people arbitrarily chosen by God – predestined to go, or not go, to hell? That would be unloving, unfair. The answer to this is that God has given us all free will to accept or refuse his offer.

God is also outside time.

He knows, from the beginning, who will accept him as their saviour, and he knows who else will be accepted in the final judgement. It is they who are the chosen ones – the 'elect'.

Those he knows, he chooses.

QUESTION 30

What is Meant By 'a New Heaven and a New Earth'?

Jesus has returned. Satan, his demons and all evil have been consigned to outer darkness. Only people whose names are written in the Lamb's book of life remain.

And God.

The promise is that the present earth and heaven will pass away at the end of time and be replaced.

There will no longer be two realms; the seen and unseen will be merged, and God and his people will be living as one. All of God's original creation will be restored and healed, as it was before the fall.

The sea, which divides and represents chaos, will disappear. There will be no tears, no mourning, crying or pain. No death.

Jerusalem – the old (man-made) holy city – will be replaced by a new city coming down from heaven – a perfect city.

It is described in symbolic terms: enormous, made of gold and shining with the glory of jewels.

It will be a place of healing and light because Jesus himself will be there.

The fruit of the tree of life, forbidden in the beginning, is given to all, for all. We shall live for ever in and with God.

We shall see God and know him face to face for ever and ever. Amen.

QUESTION 31

Who is the Holy Spirit?

A spirit is a person – not an 'it' or 'an influence'. A person but without a body. The Holy Spirit is the spirit of God – one of the Trinity – God. He has a special role of relating between God in the unseen world and our world – the seen. He has been called the 'go between God'.

In the Old Testament he is seen as hovering over the chaos in creation – bringing order, working by coming upon individuals, e.g. by giving supernatural abilities, giving artistic skills, giving power and strength to the weak, inspiring prophecy.

There are many examples of these in the Old Testament. The usual pattern was for the Holy Spirit to come, temporarily, upon an individual for a particular work God wanted performed.

In the Old Testament, God also promised that He would send out his Spirit on all flesh – male, female, young and old – giving dreams, prophetic powers and visions.

In the New Testament, Jesus talks about the Spirit in almost his last teaching to his disciples. The Greek word for the Spirit is difficult to translate into English. Literally it is 'one called alongside to help'. English translations vary: counsellor, comforter, helper, and advocate.

Jesus tells the disciples he is with them and will be in them. He will continue Jesus's teaching and it will be passed on to future generations.

He will be the one to warn of judgement and guide the world into right ways. He will speak with the authority of God and tell about things to come.

The disciples received the Holy Spirit from Jesus on the night of his resurrection. But they still lacked power. Jesus promised they would receive power when the Spirit came upon them, and at Pentecost they received this when they were baptised in the Spirit.

This happened to individuals and groups.

And it still happens today, if we allow ourselves to be immersed in the enabling and empowering work of the Holy Spirit. Christians receive power to witness, and churches grow (sometimes very rapidly) as a result. We are told to be 'filled' with the Holy Spirit (the Greek word means 'filled and refilled' – because we leak).

Individual Christians receiving baptism in the Spirit are likely to experience a renewal of their faith; a new excitement and a closer personal relationship with Jesus. The Bible will come alive; their prayer life will take on a new depth and they are likely to find themselves equipped and used powerfully by God.

There are four main areas in which the Holy Spirit works:

- bringing people into the kingdom of God;
- transforming our lives;
- giving us power;
- and creating a fellowship of love.

Read on...

QUESTION 32

What Does the Holy Spirit Do?

God wants to take over our lives by his spirit.

He wants us to grow spiritually. It is the Holy Spirit who works away in us to produce this growth and make us more like Jesus.

Most of us would lead very much happier lives on this earth if we went along with him. More love, more joy, more peace.

The early Christians were distinguished by their love for each other, which brought many people to faith in God.

The Bible talks of Christians as seeing the glory of God and being changed from one degree of glory to another. 'Glory' is what we see of the incredible beauty, power, majesty, and wonder of God as our relationship with Jesus develops.

The process has been compared to the journey a narrow boat has to make going uphill on a river, using a lock.

You approach the lock at low level – where you start. You open the gates and go in, coming just as you are.

You shut the lower gates (the past) behind you.

You open the sluices on the upper gates and let the Spirit in. Water – the Spirit – flows in – the boat rises – it doesn't even try!

The boat reaches the upper level. One more step from glory into glory.

You open the upper gates and away you go.

At a new level… towards the next lock, where it all happens again until ultimately we arrive… at Jesus.

We have the choice as to whether we want this or not. This is a work of the Holy Spirit. We need to cooperate with him in worship and prayer. We can block the process – quench the Spirit – or help him by opening our 'gates' and saying, "Yes please, Lord."

QUESTION 33

What is Baptism in the Holy Spirit?

Jesus lived a pretty normal family life as a Jewish boy in the carpenter's shop, although there is evidence that he did have a devout relationship with God – much like many Christians today. He knew the Jewish scriptures. When he was about thirty he went, with many others, to the place where John the Baptist was baptising for repentance of sins. There Jesus insisted on receiving water baptism from John.

As Jesus came up from the water, the Holy Spirit came down upon him, he received power and his ministry began – his moment of baptism in the Spirit.

After his resurrection he told his disciples that they, too, would receive the baptism of the Holy Spirit – they did. And the disciples were told to tell us! People still can receive this baptism. It is not to be confused with water baptism; the very word 'baptism' implies being drenched, immersed, and filled with the Holy Spirit.

And these are the results:

- a new intimacy with Jesus;
- a new power of prayer and praise;
- new freedom in song and worship;
- new joy in the Bible and understanding it;
- dreams and visions;
- power, freedom and confidence to tell people about Jesus;
- growing in faith, and the fruit of the Spirit;
- being used by God in new ways;
- the gifts of the Spirit.

There are nine special gifts of the Holy Spirit, which are God's toolkit for enabling us to do what he is calling us to do. They are supernatural gifts and do not depend on our own talents or abilities.

- *Speaking a word of knowledge.* Knowing something directly from God, perhaps a person's name or an illness God wants to heal, which you couldn't possibly have known by natural means.

- *Speaking a word of wisdom.* God-given wisdom at exactly the right moment when God wants to resolve a difficult situation.

- *A gift of faith.* Not the faith that makes us believers but a supernatural conviction that Jesus will reveal his power in a special way in a particular situation.

- *Gifts of healing.* Many gifts – body, mind and spirit.

- *A gift of prophecy.* Receiving and speaking or writing a direct word from God.

- *Working of miracles.* The normal currency in heaven. The releasing of God's power into a situation on earth.

- *Discernment of spirits.* Is it God's spirit or a human spirit or an evil spirit we are encountering – and, if evil, what?

- *Various kinds of tongues.* A God-given language for prayer, praise, or proclamation. Tongues come from the Spirit and not from the mind. There are four distinct kinds:

  1. A private praise and prayer language, unique for each person. You may even find you are singing it when you are on your own with Jesus.
  2. A prophetic tongue-giving, out loud, God's message to a church or a meeting.
  3. An actual foreign language not known to the speaker
  4. Singing in the Spirit – beautiful Spirit-led shared praise and worship in a group or congregation.

  Each one is a language of the Holy Spirit – beyond words – a beautiful, mysterious love language between God and the speaker which God understands.

- *Interpretation of a prophetic tongue.* This is necessary in a public or group situation, so people can know what God is saying.

All the gifts are given for the common good and to build up the church. They are God's tools for continuing Jesus's ministry on earth. They are given as and when necessary and to whom the Holy Spirit chooses. Like tools, lent out and then put back when the job is done.

A personal prayer tongue is the only one we can keep as it builds us up as well as the church.

The most usual way for someone to receive the Baptism in the Holy Spirit is through prayer and laying on of hands by someone who has already received. But it might come without asking! A wonderful experience.

If you don't know anyone to pray with you or go into more detail, ask God to show you someone. You will be surprised how soon someone – perhaps unexpectedly, perhaps on a bus or waiting in a queue – will surface.

QUESTION 34

What is 'Walking in the Spirit'?

We have an amazing God. God of power and majesty and might. God who created the universe. A God beyond our imagining.

And yet he says to you, "I created you and burn with passion for you. I burn with passionate love for each one of you."

If you are a Christian, this incredible God actually is living in you. And if you are not, he wants to come in.

He wants a relationship with you, not just on Sunday, not just in your prayer times but *all the time*. He has chosen you – yes, *you* – for a purpose. He wants to walk beside you, holding hands in everything you do – at work, at leisure, in sickness and health, in your political life, in everything, 24/7 – guiding you, steering you. And with you enjoying his company.

This is the secret of the wonderful life for which he created you. He has plans for you, plans for good – for your welfare – and not for evil.

You won't even know this is happening most of the time, but the more we can recognise it, the better everything becomes, and we too grow in our faith and amazed love for him and for others.

When we get things wrong, he transforms them, often so they are better than if we had got them right in the first place.

He is someone we can trust, who will never let us go. And we can learn to trust him.

When in doubt about anything, ask him. Learn to listen to him speaking to you in circumstances, through other people, and even by a 'voice in the back of your head'.

When you think about it, bask in that love. Swathe yourself in it.

One of the old Hebrew songs urges us to give it a trial – and find it works!

In Appendix One[1], there is an exercise you might like to try for a month. You will probably surprise yourself as you experience the Holy Spirit working in your life.

---

[1] See page 97

QUESTION 35

What is 'Fellowship in the Holy Spirit'?

We are one in the Spirit. Jesus prayed that we might be one, even as He and the Father are one.

He is in the Father and we are in him. He has given us His glory.

We have a new supernatural life in the Spirit. God wants us, passionately, to share with one another, as we develop our new relationship with the risen Lord Christ and with each other.

He wants us to experience a new joy, love and intimacy, as we learn from each other more of what Jesus has done for us.

Onlookers to the first Christians in the early church were struck by their love for one another. This is not a 'normal' relationship or friendship. It is not something with coffee and biscuits after a church service. It can, but may not, happen in a church when God opens our hearts to one another. It can happen when you meet someone on a train or at a bus stop and you both feel a deep and inexplicable love, which mirrors what Jesus has for you.

The Holy Spirit has set up the meeting.

You share, you may pray with each other, you may hug and never see them again. Or continue in contact for a lifetime.

We grow in this fellowship as we encourage each other to open ourselves to the Holy Spirit and his work in our lives.

We grow in our own private worship and with others. We grow as we learn to pray together. As we weep and laugh together. As we experiment and encourage each other to minister in the nine gifts of the Spirit, especially healing.

We grow as we give each other confidence to talk about Jesus. To share our successes and failures in our walk with him together. As we study God's word together. As we keep our focus on Jesus.

It is a life of excitement, joy and ever increasing love for each other and for those who need to know God's love. A life, being taught by the Holy Spirit, to live the new life we have been given, day by day, hour by hour. A life of riches and wonder...

It is a work of the Holy Spirit.

QUESTION 36

What is the Church?

In one discussion about who Jesus was, Peter, in a moment of sudden recognition, saw the truth. Jesus replied, saying that on this truth, he (Jesus) would build his church.

His church, not ours. His purpose was that the good news of the kingdom of God, forgiveness and love should be spread worldwide in the power of the Holy Spirit.

The Greek word translated 'church' is 'ecclesia' meaning 'people called out' for the purpose. The original church had no buildings, no Bible, and no organisation. No rules. No ministers making rules about what was, and was not, acceptable. Their sole intention was to help each other develop their relationship with the risen Lord Jesus.

They were a radiant people, excited about what had happened and what they were learning. They were to be God's instrument – his hands and feet throughout the world.

He raised up people to equip the church for special ministries – apostles, prophets, evangelists, pastors and teachers. He gave particular talents to people – serving, encouraging, generosity, helping and many others – to build the fellowship.

He gave them a great commission to go into the world, to preach the gospel, to make disciples and teach them all he had taught the original twelve.

They wouldn't have realised it but they were to be the foundation for carrying the truth of the gospel right up to our time.

Thank God for the church!

There were two problems. As the church grew, human nature began to take over with power struggles, making rules, and the like. Secondly, there was the constant attack of Satan, seeking to thwart God's plan.

The church, God's planting, had a tendency to became institutionalised, getting involved in politics and losing its way. Ritual and rules were in danger of replacing relationships with Jesus. And the church, particularly in the Middle Ages, did some terrible things, claiming them to be of God.

They would hatch up all sorts of plans from their own minds and then ask God to bless them. They lost the principle of listening for God's plans and setting out to cooperate with them.

Throughout history, God has had to step in and call them back to himself in revival and renewal. Different groups, in different countries, developed differing emphases in this process, and we are left now with a number of organisations – the denominations – each with their own traditions and part to play in preserving the faith.

They also offer a variety of forms of worship to suit different tastes. Each have their own shortcomings, but within each will be a core of godly people, loving and living in the Holy Spirit. These people are the church.

We need each other, as we share our walk with God. We are told not to neglect to assemble together to help and encourage one another in our Christian lives.

This may not always be possible where the assembly has become, for many, nothing more than a one hour service, once a week, on a Sunday.

But Jesus never said, "Come to a church service." He invited people to come to *him*.

Many local churches are discovering, once again, that Christians, new and old, need the intimacy and trust of small groups, if they are to grow in Christ.

The main Christian denominations in the UK are The Church of England (Anglicans), Methodists, Roman Catholics, Baptists, United

Reformed Church, Pentecostals, Salvation Army, Free Evangelical churches and a number of new 'community churches' and other Charismatic churches.

Any of these denominations could provide a good beginning for a new Christian, and we can thank God for them.

There are also lots of other fringe churches, some of which might not be too helpful.

Again, ask the Holy Spirit to show you.

QUESTION 37

What is Water Baptism?

Baptism is one of the 'sacraments' of the Christian church. A sacrament is an outward and visible sign of an inward and spiritual grace – a gift from God. Another definition is 'acting out on earth what God has done, or is doing, in heaven'.

Baptism has its origin in the ancient Jewish faith, when a non-Jewish person was converting to Judaism and needed to be washed clean of all their past sins.

The word 'baptism' comes from a Greek word meaning 'drench, soak, immerse'.

In the early church it was offered to new believers (and sometimes their households), retaining the idea of washing away past sins. More importantly, it took on a new symbolism. The person being baptised was totally immersed in water, representing the death and burial of their old life and then, as they emerged, resurrection into their new life in God. This is the norm in the Baptist Church, as well as a number of other churches today.

In a time of high infant mortality, the question arose, "What about babies? Will they go to heaven if not baptised?" So the ritual baptism of infants became common.

Very quickly the ritual took over and the symbol became the important thing, rather than that which was being symbolised.

We are left with two different understandings of baptism in the church.

Baptism of infants, involving sprinkling with water, is seen as a ritual of entry into the church. With this has grown up an implied threat of bad consequences if baptism doesn't happen. At its worst, that the baby will not get to heaven. Promises are made, it is sometimes claimed, 'on behalf of the child' – the parents making promises before God that the child will be brought up as a Christian in a Christian home.

Godparents and, sometimes, the congregation are also asked to make promises that they will look after the child's spiritual growth.

The hope is that he or she will come to make their own public confession of faith and complete their baptism in a service of confirmation, when they are old enough to understand.

Where infant baptism is seen as a sacrament of entry to the church – a once-only event – it can cause much heart-searching when the child is grown and wants, as a believer, to be baptised in response to God's calling.

For many today, it has become a barely understood social event, often called 'christening' (which is not a biblical term) and seen as a naming ceremony (which it is not). For more thoughtful, indeed honest, parents, unwilling to make promises before God they can't keep, there are alternative services: a thanksgiving for the birth of the child; or a dedication, presenting the child before God and praying for his protection.

'Believer's baptism', usually by total immersion at an age when the person concerned understands and chooses for themselves, is a wonderful experience. They have the opportunity to make a public statement of their faith and their acceptance of Jesus as their Saviour and Lord. And they, and the whole congregation, rejoice and receive great encouragement and blessing.

QUESTION 38

What is Holy Communion?

Some churches use the term 'the Lord's Supper', 'the Last Supper', 'the Eucharist' (meaning 'thanksgiving') or 'the Mass'.

It's the second 'sacrament' – an event initiated by Jesus for his followers on the night when he was betrayed.

He and they were celebrating the Jewish most holy annual feast of Passover – a meal where each Jewish family rehearsed how God had freed their ancestors from slavery in Egypt over a thousand years before. It recalled each of the mighty acts of the great and powerful God in that deliverance. Those present were invited to remember the history and to regard themselves as having been present when it all happened.

The sharing of bread was part of the meal – God's gift of food for their journey – some people seeing this as representing the great Messiah who was to come. There was also a ritual of drinking red wine (four glasses actually, which made it a very happy occasion).

And Jesus reinterpreted this to make the basis of what the church does today.

There are prayers of thanksgiving to God for all he has given us and, as we remember, we are taken first into praise and then deep worship. The bread and wine are symbols for all God has done for us individually and collectively. The Holy Spirit is invited to come down and make it real for us.

Jesus broke bread and shared it, saying, "Eat it, take it in, make it part of your own very self." God came to earth to rescue us. Eat it, take it in, make it part of your own very self.

God Questions

At the end of the Passover meal, the last glass of wine was like saying grace in thanksgiving for what had been received.

Jesus changed all that too. He knew he was soon going to be crucified and that his shed blood would be the ransom payment for the new relationship of freedom, love and forgiveness from God, inviting all to partake of it.

And we remember and receive and are thankful.

QUESTION 39

How Should I Pray?

Stand by to be amazed! A Christian has been given unrestricted access to God, and God loves it when we make use of it.

The medieval Bible translators have not been all that helpful in thinking about prayer. The very word has often become debased into asking God for what we want. "Give me, give me, and give me."

Prayer is all about communication with God. A conversation between two lovers: God who loves you; and you who, hopefully, are learning to love him in return. It is all a matter of relationship. It is not a matter of 'saying prayers' as a ritual, but meaning what you are feeling and thinking. And sharing it all with God.

Even the first century Church had difficulty with this, and one of the letters in the New Testament recognises this and points out that it is part of the work of the Holy Spirit to help us with our praying.

There are actually many different types of prayer:

- *Worship prayers.* Just thinking how wonderful God is.
- *Praise prayers.* Rehearsing to God, preferably out loud, the wonderful things he has done, his goodness and his everlasting love.
- *Thank you prayers.* For what he has given you.
- *Listening prayer.* Just waiting on God in silence, asking him to speak, and then paying attention to any thoughts, ideas, or pictures that occur to you.
- *Confession prayers.* Acknowledging before God and to yourself where you have got things wrong and asking him to change you. It is not a matter of asking his forgiveness – if you are a Christian you have already been forgiven at the cross. Think

about that – a miracle of love. Rejoice and share your thinking and feelings with him.

- *Asking prayers.* For what you need, for guidance and that you will remember all day that he is with you.
- *Wow prayers.* God is just so wonderful.
- *Intercessory prayers.* Praying for people, the church and the world, as God guides you. He will show you what.

It is a curious thing that when God wants to do something, he often asks us to set it in motion. He wants to us to cooperate in what *he* wants rather than asking him to cooperate with what *we* want.

Don't think there are any rules about having to do all this every time you pray. The Holy Spirit will prompt you. There is no need for the 'right' religious language. You are chatting with a lover. Any day, any time.

There are six specific promises from God that he will grant the kind of prayer that he wants prayed – the prayer that Jesus would be saying to the Father. The Holy Spirit will guide as to what that is, if you ask him.

It does help if you can set aside some time and a special place – perhaps on the commute to work, or at midmorning coffee time – as a specific prayer time.

There are some interesting questions that arise out of the Lord's Prayer. There are two slightly different versions of it in the Bible; there is no mention of 'trespasses' but one version uses 'sins' and the other 'debts'. Jesus is recorded as responding to the request of the disciples to teach them how to pray.

It was also before Jesus was crucified and took away the sin of the world.

It seems highly unlikely that Jesus wanted his followers to say – often parrot fashion and too fast even to think about it – just words like some sort of magic incantation. You can blame the medieval or earlier church for that. But we can use each section as a prompt – a model for our praying.

It starts with "Our" – we are part of a family. It recognises and worships God in heaven. It submits to his rule in our lives and in the world. Only then does it ask for anything – and that is that he will feed us. It concerns itself with forgiveness of self and others. It prays for guidance and for protection against evil. And finally ends up with the glorious chorus of praise and adoration in which, surely, the angels in heaven must join.

Go well, walking through life, holding hands with Jesus and knowing you are loved, forgiven and free.

QUESTION 40

Why is there Suffering in the World?

This is another of God's mysteries and a question asked throughout all the ages.

It may be that we have created the wrong kind of God – a sort of Father Christmas God – who should be at our beck and call in this world and let nothing bad (in our judgement) happen to us.

It may be that he did not create us for this world at all – that this world is only a preparation for the eternity in the unseen world with God, which is what he really wants. He knew what was going to have to happen.

God, the amazing and supreme artist, created this world of incredible complexity and beauty. He was delighted and thrilled with it. He then created us, in his image, and was even more thrilled with what he had done.

It is almost as if God had so much love that he simply wanted to pour it out and share it with as many million people as would accept it.

He did not create sickness, or pain or any suffering. Some sickness may come from our own sin, some from the sin of others, and much from the stresses of the modern world. These were the inevitable consequences of the choices humanity made, when tempted by Satan. .

But he did, and does, allow them to happen, to allow us to be drawn into his love and his nature. He transforms everything into good (we know not how) for those who love him. He uses our weakness in all sorts of ways. Jesus saved the world through what he suffered.

The apostle Paul prayed three times for healing of his (unknown) illness, but wasn't healed. Paul then realised two things:

- God's strength was made perfect in Paul's weakness. God was able to work through him and he didn't get in the way.
- Paul was being enabled to complete, in his suffering, what he had not understood of Jesus's suffering – the suffering of a gentle, loving, self-giving God, who gave himself for us – who is totally identified with us in this world, so that we might be so totally one with him in the real world, which is to come. Not only Lord and King, but Friend and Lover.

One other way in which we can see God working in suffering is through the compassion and love that is so often generated and enhanced among those who care for the sufferer.

As for the terrible suffering in the world – war, famine, refugees, epidemics, all the results of the giant cosmic battle raging in heavenly places – we can only pray and trust that God does know what he is doing. He is working his purposes out. For us, there remains the mystery.

But... Jesus did warn the disciples that these things would happen.

QUESTION 41

Does God Heal Today?

Healing may be defined as 'a process towards wholeness in body, soul and spirit'. Sometimes it is instantaneous and sometimes it takes time. It is not necessarily a physical cure.

Our bodies will die.

We have on record that Jesus healed on about forty occasions – some of his healings were for individuals, some for 'all who came'. He raised three people from the dead. There must have been many occasions when he did not work any supernatural healing.

Jesus never did anything unless he knew the Father was doing it. There is much mystery here, and God's thoughts and ways are very different from, and higher than, ours.

God created our bodies with a built-in healing mechanism.

God created all the discoveries of science. There is no contradiction between God's healing and that of doctors and hospitals. Both are from God.

God's healing is not the same as 'faith healing', but it seems that lack of faith can get in the way of what God wants to do.

Faith in Jesus's healing power, by the person concerned or their friends or family, seems almost to be necessary to release the healing miracle. It is faith in an almighty God to get it right. It is never a case, as some say, cruelly, when someone is not cured, that they "did not have enough faith".

Gifts of healing are included in the Bible's list of spiritual gifts, in which Spirit-led Christians are expected to cooperate with the Holy Spirit's plans (not the other way round) to do his works.

Sickness and death entered the world when mankind chose, in God's perfect creation, to 'know better than God' and to disobey him. They are the works of Satan over which Jesus triumphed on the cross.

Jesus sent his disciples out to proclaim the kingdom of God and to heal the sick and cast out demons. This they did, and this the church, when empowered by the Holy Spirit, has been doing ever since.

We are body, soul and spirit. Our spirits, dead or wounded, are totally healed when we ask Jesus into our lives and receive eternal life.

It is sometimes claimed that God's will is always that we should be totally healed in body if we ask for it. This is not true. But God will transform even sickness into something that will bring him glory.

St Paul prayed for healing three times but was not cured. He also recognised that his suffering could be to allow him to understand something of the way Jesus suffered.

He learned, too, that in his weakness he had to rely on God's power, rather than his human strength. There are many instances of this still today.

There are still some immediate cures through prayer. These can be quite dramatic and affect the sufferer and those round about as well. God often gets maximum mileage from his miracles.

The healing of the soul is a more complex matter and tends to be the focus for much of the church's healing ministry. Forgotten hurts from the past – often going back to infancy, or even earlier generations – may need healing on their own account and also because of their influence on our general health.

Many churches have prayer teams trained for this healing ministry.

Finally, illness may be the result of demonic attack. This will need specialised deliverance ministry.

QUESTION 42

What is God's View of Sex?

God created us for relationships – not just for physical pleasure. He created us male and female, to walk and talk with him, naked and unashamed, in the garden. His first command to humankind was to have sexual intercourse and thus to fill the world.

We were to experience the closest relationship possible between two people, literally entered into bodily union and the totality of surrender to each other in orgasm. Physical and emotional. Lost in love. The two were to become one flesh – one self. And this was to become productive in fulfilling God's purposes.

Sexuality was one of God's most intimate and wonderful original gifts to mankind and a foretaste of the spiritual relationship God designed us for in relationship with him. A relationship of total self-giving, total surrender, total joy and satisfaction.

It is no coincidence that, right at the end of the Bible and of time, when Jesus returns, the analogy is one of a wedding feast with Jesus, the Lamb of God marrying his bride – the church – and the consummation of all things in God. At which point, in the new heaven and new earth, there ceases to be any male and female. Our sexuality has done its job.

Like everything else, this was lost in man's disobedience and the fall, and God's precious gift became a problem.

What happens when promiscuous sex leads to people becoming more than 'one flesh'? Jealousy, AIDS, adultery, family breakdown, children with a series of multiple fathers and no role models all result. The apostle, Paul, condemns becoming 'one flesh' with a prostitute.

Maybe God got it right in the first place.

QUESTION 43

So What Happens When You Believe?

So you decide to believe, or realise that you do believe that...

- Jesus is the Son of God;
- he came to this earth;
- what he says is true;
- he died on the cross to take away our sin;
- he rose again from the dead;
- and he returned to his Father, where he reigns forever in God's kingdom.

You may find yourself doubting some of this occasionally, but don't worry; God has got you and he will never let you go.

So what happens?

- Angels in heaven rejoice.
- The Holy Spirit comes into you and takes up residence. Christ is in you and you are in him.
- Your spirit, which was dead because of your sins, is given a new life in Jesus. Your body will die but the real you – your soul and spirit – will live forever with God in heaven from that moment.
- All your sins – past, present and future – are totally forgiven. God does not even remember them.
- You become a child of God, adopted into his family.
- You are set free from the curse of trying to be good enough for heaven. Actually you can't ever be good enough. But Jesus gives you *his* righteousness (which means 'right relationship with God').

- The Holy Spirit will begin the process of cleaning you up and sorting you out. It is the beginning of a wonderful and exciting journey. It takes you ultimately into the very likeness of Jesus.
- You will find a new community of amazing love among God's people.

If you look in Appendix Two[2], you will find thirty-three Bible references, all of which apply to you!

---

[2] Page 99

QUESTION 44

What Does 'Grace' Mean?

The best definition of grace is 'undeserved favour'. It is God's favour and blessing – and we don't deserve it.

Some people like to use idea of 'God's Riches At Christ's Expense'.

In Old Testament days, before Jesus came, receiving God's blessing was very much conditional on good behaviour by his people. If you kept God's laws – preferably all of them – God would be pleased with you, you would win battles, you would have good harvests. And, if not, not.

The sad thing is that these ideas have crept into Christian thinking. We hear over and over at funerals how good and lovely the person was, with the unspoken suggestion that they were good enough to earn a place in heaven.

If you ask many Christians if they will be in heaven, the most common answer is, "I hope so."

In the New Testament, after Jesus's resurrection, the Law is presented as a schoolmaster teaching us something – as sinful people, albeit forgiven. We simply *cannot* be good enough to earn God's love and blessing – and a place in heaven when we die.

Jesus's message was different: we need a new way of thinking. God offers us a free gift: Jesus, the son of God; Jesus without sin. Jesus, out of love for humankind, when he died on the cross, took into himself every sin, failure and everything separating us from God. He took all the punishment we deserve. He offers us new lives – of love, of joy, of peace – and eternal life in and with him.

Only believe and receive.

QUESTION 45

What Does It Mean to Be 'In Christ'?

Are you 'in Christ'? If you believe in Jesus, Son of God, who died on the cross for your sin, who rose again from the dead, and if you have in any way committed your life to him...

...then you are in Christ.

It is not a matter of being good enough; we can't be. We are free from all the laws and rules. It is sheer grace – God's undeserved love – to all who believe.

There are scores of passages in the New Testament about what this means. They make up the most important description and guidance for the Christian journey, discipleship and victory.

Do you realise...

...Christ is in *you* – a mystery – the hope (certainty) of glory? Jesus, the Christ, by whom and for whom all the galaxies were created, actually dwells in you, by the Holy Spirit. Your body is a temple of the Holy Spirit.

Jesus, in the cross and resurrection, broke Satan's power. From the tomb, he rose from death and broke the power of death.

In Christ we are a totally new creation. By faith, we participate in Jesus's death and resurrection. We are born again, new creatures, children of God.

All your sins, past, present and future have been taken away, borne by Jesus, the sinless one, on the cross. You are forgiven. Yes, you will go on doing bad things and thinking bad thoughts, because you still live in your old self's body, which contains the remnants of sin; but *sin no longer rules over you.*

You are set free from your old nature; there is *no* condemnation by God for you. You are no longer defined as a sinner – still less as a 'miserable sinner' – desperately trying to live a godly and holy life.

You don't have to go on, repeatedly, asking God to forgive you; He already has.

Most of us have habitual patterns of sinful attitudes and actions resulting from our past – needs that long to be satisfied but never seem to be. We need to acknowledge these (that is what 'confess' means) and pray, not to be forgiven but to give thanks that we are, and ask God to sort us out.

The Greek word translated 'repent' in the Bible, 'metanoia', means to 'have a completely new head and heart'; this is what we need continually to ask the Lord for. We are not told to transform ourselves but to *be* transformed. This is where the Holy Spirit comes in.

A butterfly starts as a wriggly caterpillar, then is transformed into a 'dead' chrysalis, which then becomes the beautiful creature we see flying in the garden. It does not have to spend its life trying to change.

The process is called metamorphosis, which is the word in the Bible for the change brought about by the Holy Spirit – changing us towards, and ultimately into, the very image of Christ. And we do need to ask for this, to learn to listen to his voice, to follow his promptings, and to try not to get in his way.

This becomes easier once you have really taken in who you are in Christ. Stop trying, learn to listen to the Holy Spirit, and let the Holy Spirit take control and transform your life for you.

Beloved child of God, know who you are in Christ. Cling to him. Cultivate your relationship with him. Jesus said we should abide in him; stay there, rest there.

With him you have a new nature, infused with Christ's life and power.

QUESTION 46

What is Witnessing?

Jesus said to his friends that they would become his witnesses, ultimately to the end of the earth. But he told them to wait to receive that power.

A witness is someone who has experienced something and tells others about it – like in a courtroom.

It is not someone giving their opinion or trying to explain something to others. Still less is it trying to persuade others of your point of view.

The witness of Christian people is a powerful weapon in God's armoury. People may think you are mad but they can't argue with what you have experienced with God.

A few weeks after Jesus was raised from the dead, the Holy Spirit did come upon the disciples, as promised, and their witness to the crowd in Jerusalem brought three thousand people into faith.

Incidentally, the Greek word 'martyr' – someone killed for their faith – means 'witness', but mercifully, we are not all called to that.

Neither are most of us called to make converts to the Christian faith; that is the job of the Holy Spirit.

But all Christians are called always to be ready to give an account for the reason we believe. What God has done for me? How has God changed me?

You may need to practice this with Christian friends. It will give you confidence next time someone asks why you go to church or why you believe all that religion stuff. The evidence you give may change someone's life.

APPENDIX ONE

Life to Share – Life in the Spirit

The aim is to focus, for a week at a time, on one of the aspects of walking in the Spirit so that the experiences of the Lord during that week might be built into our subsequent walk.

I believe what follows is something the Lord wants of me. It may – or may not – be for others. Like so much of life in the Spirit, it is an experiment. An exercise in trust.

Begin where you are now. Forgiven, in the kingdom, growing in sanctification, equipped with all the gifts and every spiritual blessing, surrendered to God to use as he wills. Jesus is the centre of all our life.

Week 1. Prayer in the Spirit.

Abandon all previous patterns of 'quiet times' and create/make time daily – perhaps half or one hour – and commit it to God, expecting him to fill it.

- This in itself is an act of praise and trust and worship.
- Pray about any distractions and preoccupations as they arise.
- Listen to God and do what He says immediately.
- If 'nothing happens', just wait, basking in being loved as the servant watching the master's hand (see Psalm 123) and ready for any gesture or instructions.

If you have any thoughts or ideas which might come from God about what to do, e.g. to read a passage from the Bible, lie down on the floor, light a candle, look up a book (perhaps a commentary, Bible daily notes or other devotional reading), or make a list of people and pray for them, *do it immediately.*

Keep a detailed journal for the week.

Week 2. At home in the Spirit.

Commit the day to God and expect him to take it on. What does God want you to do today? Ask him. If you have any thoughts or ideas that might come from God, *follow them up immediately* – e.g. write them down, phone or email people, clean the loo, mow the lawn, go out for a walk, etc. When? *Ask him*, and if you hear or think a specific time, *do it then*.

Week 3. Going out in the Spirit.

Commit your outing to God and expect him to do things in it. Where does he want you to go? When? Whom does he want you to meet or talk to? Ask him to arrange this. If you get talking to someone – friend or stranger – why has God set this up? *Ask him*. If you get any sense of an answer that is possibly from a loving God, *do it*.

Week 4. Praising in the Spirit.

Commit each day to God and expect him to work for good in everything that happens (see Romans 8.28).

Praise God for what he is doing in everything – every frustration, red traffic light, computer failure, your own or other people's failures – praise him. The good bits and the bad.

For every angry thought or aggressive feeling – praise him.

For every pain, illness, tiredness – praise him.

And share the results with someone.

APPENDIX TWO

33 Bible Quotes that Apply to All Christians

In Christ I am accepted

John 1:12	I am God's child.
John 15:15	I am Christ's friend.
Romans 5:1	I have been justified.
1 Corinthians 6:17	I am united with the Lord and I am one spirit with Him.
1 Corinthians 6:20	I have been bought with a price. I belong to God.
1 Corinthians 12:27	I am a member of Christ's body.
Ephesians 1:1	I am a saint.
Ephesians 1:5	I have been adopted as God's child.
Ephesians 2:18	I have direct access to God through the Holy Spirit.
Colossians 1:14	I have been redeemed and forgiven of all my sins.
Colossians 2:10	I am complete in Christ.

I am secure

Romans 8:1,2	I am free from condemnation.
Romans 8:28	I am assured that in all things God works together for good.
Romans 8:31-34	I am free from any condemning charges against me.
Romans 8:35-39	I cannot be separated from the love of God.
2 Corinthians 1:21,22	I have been established, anointed and sealed by God.
Colossians 3:3	I am hidden with Christ in God.
Philippians 1:6	I am confident that the good work God has begun in me will be perfected.
Philippians 3:20	I am a citizen of heaven.
2 Timothy 1:7	I have not been given a spirit of fear, but of power, love and a sound mind.

Hebrews 4:16	I can find grace and mercy and help in time of need.
1 John 5:18	I am born of God and the evil one cannot touch me.

I am significant

Matthew 5:13,14	I am the salt and light of the earth.
John 15:1,5	I am a branch of the true vine, a channel of his life.
John 15:16	I have been chosen and appointed to bear fruit.
Acts 1:8	I am a personal witness of Christ.
1 Corinthians 3.16	I am God's temple.
2 Corinthians 5:17-21	I am a minister of reconciliation.
2 Corinthians 6:1	I am God's co-worker (see 1 Corinthians 3:9).
Ephesians 2:6	I am seated with Christ in the heavenly realm.
Ephesians 2:10	I am God's workmanship.
Ephesians 3:12	I may approach God with freedom and confidence.
Philippians 4:13	I can do all things through Christ who strengthens me.

These verses were selected in the published booklet 'Ministering the Steps to Freedom in Christ' by Dr Neil T Anderson. Copyright for the booklet has now passed to the Baker Publishing Group. Reproduction here is under the Group's fair use policy, for which written permission is not required.